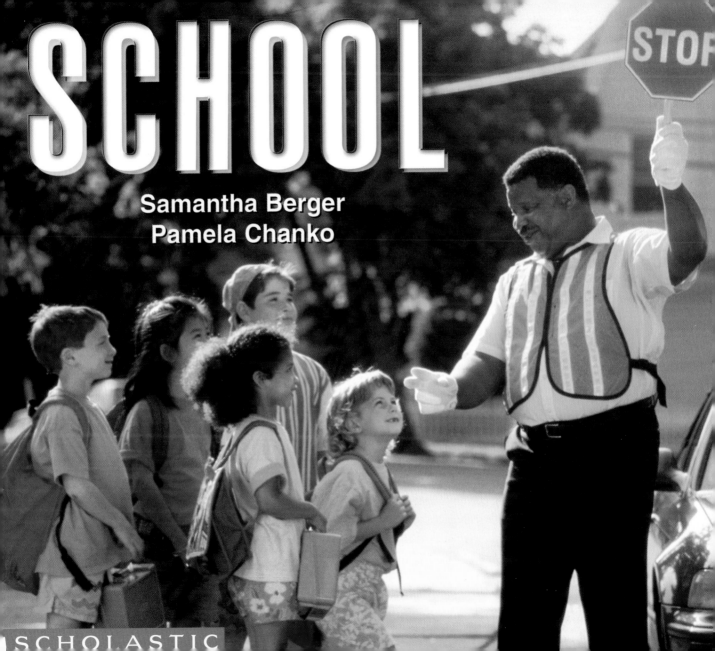

SCHOOL

Samantha Berger
Pamela Chanko

STOP

SCHOLASTIC

SCHOOL

Samantha Berger • Pamela Chanko

Scholastic Inc.

New York • Toronto • London • Auckland • Sydney

Acknowledgments

Literacy Specialist: Linda Cornwell

Social Studies Consultant: Barbara Schubert, Ph.D.

Design: Silver Editions

Photo Research: Silver Editions

Endnotes: Jacqueline Smith

Endnote Illustrations: Anthony Carnabucia

—————————————————

Photographs: Cover: R. Hutchings/Photo Edit; p. 1: Jeffry Myers/The Image Works; p. 2: Richard Hutchings Photo/Photo Researchers, Inc.; p. 3: Chris Cheadle/Tony Stone Images; p. 4: Frank Siteman/The Picture Cube, Inc.; p. 5: Michael Newman/Photo Edit; p. 6: Gabe Palmer/The Stock Market; p. 7: Jaques Chenet/Woodfin Camp & Assoc.; p. 8: Margaret Miller/Photo Researchers, Inc.; p. 9: R. Hutchings/Photo Edit; p. 10: Robert E. Daemmrich/Tony Stone Images; p. 11: David Lissy/The Picture Cube, Inc.; p. 12: Ken Karp.

Library of Congress Cataloging-in-Publication Data
Berger, Samantha.
School/Samantha Berger, Pamela Chanko.
p. cm.--(Social studies emergent readers)
Summary: Simple text and photographs explore the people in a school community, including teachers, children, librarians, nurses, and bus drivers.
ISBN 0-439-04553-3 (pbk.: alk. paper)
1. Elementary schools--Juvenile literature. 2. Elementary schools--Pictorial works--Juvenile literature.
[1. Schools.] I. Chanko, Pamela, 1968-. II. Title. III. Series.
LB1556.B47 1999
372--dc21   99-26319
                                                                                                              CIP

4   5   6   7   8   9   10   08   03   02   01   00   99

In a school, people work together.

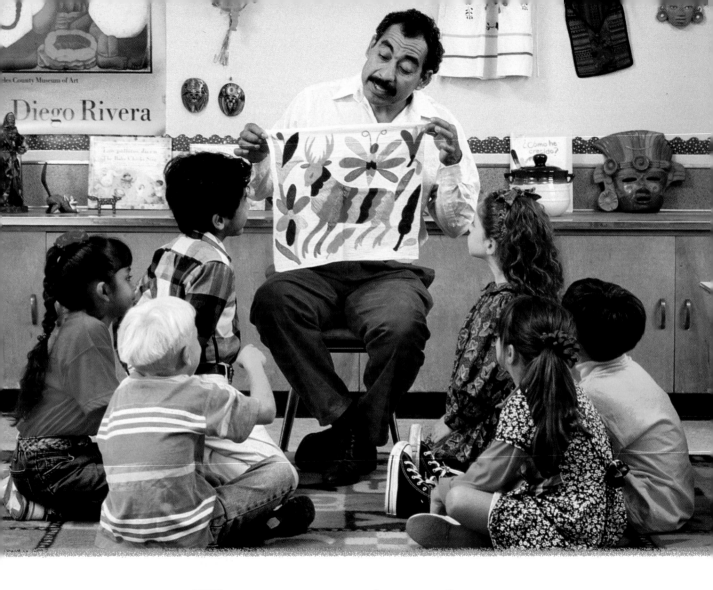

There are teachers,

and there are children.

There are librarians,

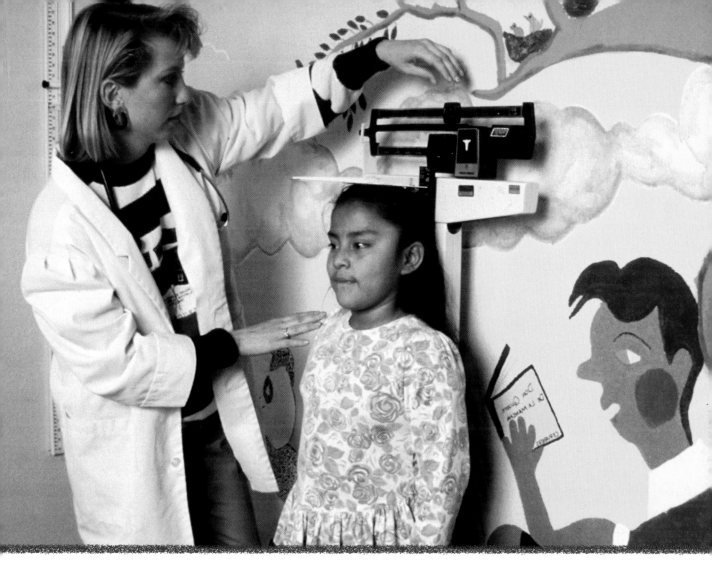

and there are nurses.

There are art teachers,

and there are dance teachers.

There are bus drivers,

and there are crossing guards

There are parents,

and there are visitors.

A school is a community.

SCHOOL

A community is a group of people who work together for a purpose. In schools that purpose is education. Everyone in the school community does a different job to ensure that children are successful in school and later in life.

Teachers Classroom teachers have to have a lot of energy and love for their work. They plan lessons, explain ideas, listen to children, answer questions, show students how to do things, read stories, and let parents know about their children's progress. They do this each and every year with new classes of children.

Children Children are the focus of the school community. They work very hard, too. They practice writing letters, words, sentences, and, eventually, stories and essays. They learn to do arithmetic. They read a lot. They do experiments to understand science. They exercise and play sports. It's hard work, but it's fun!

Librarians Librarians also have an important job in the school. They help students find information, recommend good books to read, and teach children how to use the library. Nowadays, many school libraries are called media centers because they contain several kinds of media such as audiobooks, videotapes, CD-ROMs, and computers.

Nurses Not all schools have nurses, but in those that do, the school nurse watches out for everyone's health during the school day. Children go to the nurse when they don't feel well. The nurse can treat minor injuries—for example, putting ice on a bruise. And if anyone in the school needs emergency care, the nurse is ready to administer first aid.

Art teachers Art teachers help children to enjoy creating, looking at, and thinking about art. In art class children learn how to make shapes, mix colors, draw, paint, and sculpt. They learn about art from other countries and other times.

Dance teachers Dance teachers help children learn how to move their bodies to music. Sometimes they teach specific movements, and sometimes they let children make up their own! Dance teachers understand how the body works and moves, and they are familiar with different kinds of music.

Bus drivers Bus drivers have the important job of getting children safely to and from school. They drive very carefully and watch what the children are doing. School buses in the United States are bright yellow because it is the easiest color to see and the black letters stand out.

Crossing guards Crossing guards also get children safely to and from school. They stand at intersections in the rain, snow, or hot sun. They direct traffic and watch the children and parents cross the streets. Crossing guards wear uniforms and sometimes use a whistle to direct traffic.

Parents Parents are very important to children's education. Parents are their children's first teachers, but their job does not end when children start going to school. Parents make sure that their children have all the things they need for school every day. They check that their children do homework, and sometimes they help. They also meet with the teachers.

Visitors The school community is part of the larger outside community—the neighborhood, the city, the country, and the world. Visitors sometimes come to schools to teach children things that will help them to live in the larger community.

Social Studies

EMERGENT READERS

A school is a special community.
Find out who is a part of it.

ISBN 0-439-04553-3